"Downtown"

These memories are based on life in the   s
of the area.

> "In those days you could buy anything in Commercial Road - ...re were shops for everything."

> "Commercial Road was just as though it was a bank holiday in the evening - there were hundreds of people about although the shops closed at 7pm or 8pm - or 9pm on a Saturday. It was full of life down there; people walked about to look in the shop windows which were all lit up. If there were any fights they were just fist fights and if a policeman came along he gave them a cuff, shoved them off and that was the end of it."

> "In the evening there used to be hundreds of people about along Commercial Road and under the railway bridge. All the young boys and girls used to be along there 'clicking' each other. The 'monkies' walk' they used to call it. The potato man used to be along there with his truck selling hot potatoes, and hot chestnuts and so on."

> "You never felt lonely in Commercial Road of an evening. Everyone and anyone was about. At night it wasn't dark because we had all the advertising lights - like Piccadilly Circus. It was bright with adverts for soup and all sorts - not a miserable dark place like it is now."

We start our 'walk' along the road on the west side, at the southern end using the Kelly's directories of the twenties as a guide. Where there are gaps in the street numbers we have omitted private houses.

1-13 Built as **Portsmouth Protestant Institute** by H.Jones. The architects were E.J.Smith and W.Yeardye. The halls were opened on the 24th of February 1886. The large hall held up to 2,000 people. By 1890 the name had changed to the **Albert Hall**. Entertainment included boxing matches, magic lantern shows and in 1912 moving pictures. The halls were demolished in 1936 and Commercial Chambers now occupies the site.

1 **Madame Vernon**, dress agency later **Dashwood & Sons**, funeral directors.

3 **The Albert Hall**

"The Albert Hall had tip-top dances at first but then the sailors got in there and the foreign sailors and then they'd have to send for the police and the navy police and frog march the leaders up the road. That was in the thirties and at that time the Albert Hall had a bit of a funny name - mind you, what dance hall didn't?"

5 **Carminati & Spinelli**, confectioners.

7-9 Was for at least fifty years a surgical belt maker, first **Andersons** and later **Lindsey & Sons**.

"They made corsets and trusses and artificial legs. As kids we used to look in the shop, hoping no one was looking. They made leg irons too - quite a lot of kids had to wear leg irons - there was a lot of rickets about then. They used to know what gave you rickets and they used to give you cod liver oil for it."

11 **National Cash Register Co. Ltd.**

"Most shops didn't have a cash register then, they just had a wooden box to keep their money in. They certainly didn't have ones that add up and everything like the fancy ones today."

13 **Mrs Eliza Dunkin**, The Servants Registry Office

"My sisters used to go there to get a job. There were no fees, they were glad to get them. A lot of girls from the orphanages went into service."

15 Contained the offices of various accountancy and insurance companies.

17 **Parker & Co.**, Fancy goods warehouse on the ground floor with a dental surgery above.

"People wouldn't go to the dentist in those days until they had terrible toothache, they were places you avoided until the very last moment. If you had a toothache you would use oil of cloves, iodine or whisky. Another thing I used to use was a little shred of tobacco in the hole, that stopped the pain. You would do anything rather than go to the dentist."

19 **Army Recruiting Office**, more about that when we look at the Victoria Hall on the opposite side of the road.

21 **Frederick May**, confectioner

> "He sold a lot of chocolate, it was good stuff, special. He was a big man and always had a white apron on in the shop. We could never afford his sweets he had in there, they were what used to be called hand made."

23 **William Beal**, Oyster Bar.

> "We used to go there for oyster shells to crush up for the fowls. Oyster shells were used for all kinds of things, they were crushed up and used with egg whites for setting stones into jewellery. They were also used for making terrazzo, like artificial marble, for shop doorways. It was a mixture of granite chippings, oyster shells and fish scales and they would grind it smooth to get that marble effect."

Here was Ordnance Court

25 **Mrs Louisa Creamer**, fruiterer.

27 **Mrs Paterson**, tobacconist.

29 **Newnham & Co.**, Gun Makers.

> "They sold shot guns, sporting guns and rifles. People who were interested and could afford to buy such things went there. Shotguns were sold mainly to farmers and sporting guns to the well off who could afford such an expensive hobby."

31 **The Gem**, listed in the trade directories as a beer retailer from 1855 to 1875. Named in the 1887 directory. It was later a Portsmouth United Breweries house and was demolished in 1969.

33 **Robert Moore**, Confectioner.

> "There were lots of sweets that we don't see now, dusties were my favourites. There were lots of little sweet makers then. Burchells had a shop in New Road and Maynards made sweets in Commercial Road, and Hostlers in Cosham Street. There was a shop in Charlotte Street where you could look in the window and see the man working the rock, pulling it out and pulling it out. As children we stood there for hours watching him."

Here were St. Michael's Cottages. Earlier known as Gibb's Court.

35 Maurice Kauffman, *jewellers. Originally Kauffman, tobacconist, and before that a beer retailer from 1875 to 1890, named The Lion in the 1887 directory.*

37-41 The Golden Fleece, rebuilt in 1867 it dates back to at least 1844 in the directories. It was a Simmond's house. It was demolished in 1971.

43 Mrs Emily Isted, Antique Dealer, Glass and China Repairer.

"They actually used to make glass there, he used to blow the glass and make all kinds of things. He made bottles and vases and glass flowers and all sorts. I remember it because we took a clock there, it was a special one and we took it there to get a bit of glass made."

"They used to repair china with glue or wires. It was not unusual to see china repaired in that way. In those days people were poorer and if a family had good things they were handed down and looked after and repaired. If you had something that belonged to your grandmother and it got broken, you naturally had it mended because of the sentimental value."

45-47 Royal Naval Orphanage

"It was a nice looking building and it had lovely arches in it and ivy all over. You went through a brickwall with this archway in it and along a path with trees and grass right down to the house. It really was a nice building. The boys and girls used to be fetched out for walks and they used to march along in two's. They had red and blue uniforms. Most of the boys went into the navy or one of the services and the girls usually went into service."

49 Woolwich Buildings, another office block with solicitors and building society offices.

51 Mrs Hettie Zalusky, tobacconist.

53 Joseph Carminati, confectioner.

55 L.L.Waters & Co., typewriter repairers.

57 Hall, Pain and Goldsmith, Estate Agents to the War Department. Was Ernest Hall and later became Hall, Pain and Foster.

St. Michael's Cottages

59 The Great Western, listed in the trade directories from 1878. It was rebuilt in 1902 to the designs of local architect A.E.Cogswell and was a Portsmouth United Breweries house. It was demolished in 1972.

61 Arthur Tyler, hairdresser.

63 Continental Cafe and Restaurant, owned and run by Bartholomew Albertolli & Sons.

> "Before the Indian and Chinese restaurants came in we used to do curry. We had a chef whose speciality was curry, he made a proper one and it would take him all night to make it. Portsmouth people, having been abroad a lot of them, appreciated it. We did French food .... Weiner Schnitzel ... we brought continental cooking to Portsmouth when my father and uncle came to Commercial Road in the 1890's. In the window of the restaurant we always had a 56lb Chocolate Menière, a French chocolate. In the old days ladies used to eat a lot of chocolate and we used to whip it up frothy with a stick in the French manner. We had a big block in the window and people didn't believe it was real. I used to eat a piece to show it was real. We had big lumps of beef in the window too!"

> "The outside was all teak and very ornamental. The windows were all shaped and although it wasn't very wide it was very imposing. An ordinary Portsmouth person would look twice at it as to whether to go in because you would think it was too posh for you - too high class."

65 Monck's Oyster Bar, later taken over by the Albertolli's.

> "Monck's was very famous. Being in the middle of town it drew all the best people. You stood at the counter and had oysters and champagne, or stout and winkles if you liked, with thin bread and butter. Oysters were half a crown a dozen then. Colchesters - they were the best - were four shillings a dozen. I think they are about £1 a pound now."

67 Insurance Office

69 Southdown Motor Services Ltd., bus proprietors.

Here was Swan Yard Passage

The Great Western

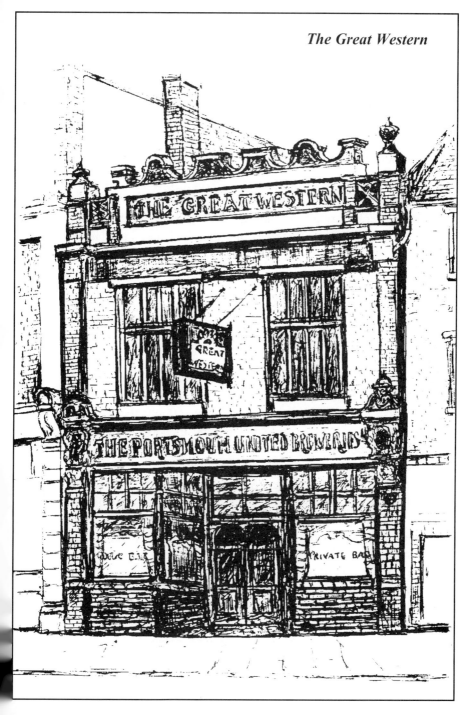

71 **The White Swan** resembles the Air Balloon at the other end of Commercial Road, they were designed by the same local architect, A.H.Bone. It dates back to at least 1823 in the trade directories and has had many variations on its name, plain White Swan, Tavern and Inn and in 1865 White Swan & Theatre Tavern and was originally a Garrett's house. As well as changing name it has had several addresses, Cold Harbour, Spring Row, Landport Road and finally Commercial Road. The present building dates from 1906. It was much used for club and society meetings in the large lounge. On the first floor was a 'gentlemans room' for the use of the landlords select guests.

> "The White Swan used to have a very fine collection of theatrical postcards. All the actors and theatrical people used to go in there while they were waiting to go on stage. All the big names used to go in there and leave their photographs and that, and they had them behind the bar."

The Theatre Royal

The site was originally the Landport Racquet Hall built in 1800. It became the Landport Theatre in 1854. The doorway to the adjacent White Swan was bricked up and the building converted to the New Theatre Royal, opening on the 29th of September 1856 with two new plays; "A New Way to Pay Old Debts" and "Founded On Facts". Alterations were made to the theatre in 1868 and 1874. In 1884 it was substantially rebuilt to the designs of C.J.Phipps with a stage 56 feet wide and 36 feet deep. In May 1900 the theatre was closed for major alterations, the stage was set back and increased to 65 feet deep, the auditorium was enlarged by the addition of extra boxes and the familiar cast iron balcony and canopy added. The architect for this scheme was another well known theatre architect Frank Matcham. The theatre re-opened in August 1900 with the play "Magda". In March 1932 the theatre opened as a cinema with the film "Common Law"; back projection was used because of the depth of the stage. In September 1948 the building reverted to being a theatre until 1956 when it became the venue for wrestling bouts. In 1968 the pantomime from the King's was transferred here for an extended run. The theatre then closed and apart from brief use as a film set was not used. On the 29th of September 1972 a fire started by vandals burnt out the stage and backstage accommodation. Later more vandalism destroyed large areas of the decorative plasterwork. Happily the theatre has now been rescued by the Theatre Royal Trust. It has been rerofed and most of the plasterwork replaced and occasional performances are now held using a temporary stage inside the auditorium.

"The Theatre Royal was the place for all the dramas. They had all the big plays there, tragedies and so on. Afterwards the theatre started to go down and they altered it into a cinema but that only lasted fifteen or so years and then they made it a wrestling hall. Ken Russell made 'The Boyfriend' there and they painted all over the front. It's being cleaned off at the moment (1981)."

Prudential Buildings

Built in 1891 to the designs of Alfred Waterhouse, four storeys of red brick and red-brown terracotta rise to steeply stepped gables. The local architects G.Rake and A.E.Cogswell had their offices here. Other local architects A.Bone and V.Inkpen also practised in the area. Has housed at various times the offices of insurance companies, solicitors, an Enquiry Agent, and the Vice Consul of the Republic of Latvia. It also housed Underwoods School of Shorthand and Typing.

"In those days people who wanted to get on in their jobs had to go to night school in their own time. We nearly all left school at fourteen and had to take what job we could. Underwoods did training for office work and you could go there during the day if your parents were able to pay. But they did evening classes too in typing and shorthand and so on."

77 **De Vere & Co.**, tobacconists.

79 **Freemasons' Club**

"If you weren't in it you didn't know what they did. It was a business-man's lodge - all the big businessmen and the Lord Mayors and such belonged. They used to say if you were a mason up on a charge they'd give you a nod and a wink and you was off!"

81 **The Nine Elms**, listed as a beer retailer in the 1859 directory it is first named in 1863. It was a Lush's house and closed in 1971. After standing derelict for some years it was renovated along with the Waterloo next door and reopened as a night club.

83 **The Waterloo**, listed as a beer retailer in the 1874 directory, named from 1887. It was a Simmond's house. It closed in 1976.

85 **Tom Scott-Foster and Edward Foster**, dental surgeons.

> "Most dentists then had foot operated drills. Nobody went for six monthly check-ups like they do today. A lot of people went to the hospital - it cost half a crown to have a tooth out but in hospital it was free. There was no gas, a cocaine injection if you were lucky but often they just yanked it out. There was no telling you about not eating sweet stuff or about cleaning your teeth. Some people used to rub their teeth with a mixture of soot and salt on a clean piece of rag. I didn't then know what a toothbrush looked like!"

87 **Portsea Island Gas Light Co.**, on the corner of Park Road, originally a red brick building, rebuilt in 1915 in white stone. Note the plaque in Park Road.

> "When I was a boy, on Friday afternoon I used to take the registers from Bramble Road School down to the Technical College to hand them in. On the north wall of the Gas Company you'll see a special engraved plaque commemorating the opening and I distinctly remember the mason doing that particular block. I believe he made an error on the last word and if you look closely you'll find the stonework has been corrected."

Behind the Gas Office were the Corporation and Fire Station stables.

On the other corner of Park Road stood the Townhall. This was the site of the first free public library in Portsmouth, opened in 1858 in a building formerly occupied by the commander of the Royal Artillery.

> "The start was made with 2,000 volumes... the library and reading room were kept open until 10 o'clock so as to allow young men employed in business, there was no early closing in those days, a chance of seeing the periodicals of the day."

The Townhall

The site was purchased from the War Department in 1883 for £10,000. The foundation stone was laid on the 14th of August 1886 by Mayor A.S.Blake. The architect was William Hill of Leeds, who was also responsible for Bolton and Leeds Townhalls and the cost of building and fitting out was £138,000. The Townhall was opened on the 9th of August 1890 by T.R.H. The Prince and Princess of Wales. When it was opened the Prince of Wales said:

"You have every right to feel proud of this fine building, worthy of the largest naval port in the United Kingdom. I sincerely trust that the deliberations which will take place within in its walls may tend to promote the welfare and prosperity of the town."

On the 21st of April 1926 it became the Guildhall. During 1939 the offices were modified, the ceilings and walls strengthened and the ground floor corridors shored up and sand-bagged. On the night of the 10th of January 1941 the building was burnt out by incendiary bombs. In 1951 B.Webber was appointed architect for reconstruction which was started on the 23rd of April 1955 by Messrs Gee, Walker & Slater. The cost of rebuilding was £864,531. H.M. the Queen re-opened the Guildhall on the 8th of June 1959. The main hall seats 2,000 and is equipped with a large Compton organ.

"In those days the Townhall held the Police and all sorts. In 1920 there was Education, Treasurers, Police, Health Offices, Coroners Office, Borough Engineer, Tramways, Telephones, Old Age Pension Committee, Public Assistance Committee and the Mental Deficiency Act Commissioners."

"When the police had a station in the Guildhall, the urchins would wait for them to come marching out, Indian file, on the way to their beats, with their capes slung over their shoulders and led by the sergeant. They would dance alongside singing that well known policeman song and there wasn't a lot the poor bobbies could do about it except out of the corner of their mouths they would mutter 'Go On, Clear Off!'."

The Townhall, now the Guildhall, faced the Square.

"The Square at one time used to be a great place for free speech. They used to hold a lot of meetings down there - political meetings and religious meetings. It was Portsmouth's Hyde Park Corner and you could get down there and have a good argument. I remember the Blackshirts down there. Where Queen Victoria's monument was would be the Labour Party and preachers and so on all speaking and the Blackshirts started coming down and standing there with their arms folded. They had a branch in Portsmouth and they weren't stopped until Mosley was put in prison or where ever it was they put him."

"I remember being in the Square on V.E. night - we were there 'til 5 o'clock in the morning. All the flag poles were up - they greased them to stop people climbing up them, and the square was absolutely packed. The old wooden gates from the goods station were piled on the bonfire in the middle of the square with any other combustible material in the vicinity. Of course Queen Victoria's statue was on the other side of the square and there were bus shelters in the middle of the road. Buses, trolley-buses and all sorts of traffic went through then."

Alongside the Townhall is the 1914-18 War Memorial, foundation stone was laid on the 25th of May 1921 and it was completed by the 19th of October in the same year. Behind the Townhall was the Municipal College the foundation stone of which was laid on the 22 of July 1904. It opened in 1908 and was designed by the local architect G.Smith.

"Anyone learning a trade went to the Municipal College or the Technical School it was sometimes called. If you were doing a fully fledged apprenticeship then you went so many days a week but most people had to go to night classes. I did a bricklaying apprenticeship. We would do all the plans and drawings in the college and then on, I think, a Tuesday afternoon we would go to tin huts in Marylebone Street and try it all out. We used to build arches, piers, bulls-eye windows, all types of brickwork, all with lime mortar so we could knock it all down again and put the mortar back into the bin to be used the following week."

"The town mortuary used to be down the side of the Guildhall and the bodies used to be laid out on stone slabs to keep cool. I've heard that sometimes when a train went past into the Town Station, the vibration used to roll the bodies off the slabs!"

On the other side of the Townhall, just before the railway arch, were some notorious public toilets.

"You went down some steps and inside was all tiled but -phew! - you had to hold your nose."

"On the railway embankment there were all trees, lovely trees they were and one or two were unusual for this part of the country. At the foot of the embankment was **Verrecchia's Ice Cream Parlour**. You walked in and went up some steps and there were tables with beautifully carved high backed settles - there is one now in the City Museum. You could have a lovely cup of coffee or a beautiful ice cream. If you

12

wanted it outside you went round the side and got a cornet for a penny, a knicker-bocker glory was a shilling."

"Under the railway bridge there used to be a subway and before they had the drainage done it used to flood every time it rained. Us kiddies used to go there and watch people trying to get through. Sometimes there would be water up to Stanhope Road."

Between the railway arch and Stanhope Road was the Head **Post Office and Telegraph Office**. Built in 1881 the architect was E.G.Rivers of H.M. Office of Works and Public Buildings, the builders were Messrs Steven & Son. It was built of rusticated brickwork and schalk stone, a brown stone. It was extended in 1896. The mosaic floor of the posting hall featured sea creatures. The building was demolished in 1978.

"People didn't have telephones then and if you wanted to get a message to someone you had to telegraph them. You wrote out what you wanted sent and they used a key to send the message through in Morse code - like in the Westerns. The girl the other end wrote it down and the telegraph boys delivered it on their bikes."

"Before the war we had four deliveries a day and even during the war we had three. They were about 7.30 in the morning, one at 9 o'clock, one at about 11.30 and one in the afternoon. You could write a letter to a friend inviting them to tea that afternoon and it would be delivered in time. The postmen always wore their uniforms. They were blue then, not grey, and I can just remember when they wore a cap with a peak front and back. A lot had bicycles with wicker basket on the front and there were always lots of telegraph boys about too. A letter was a penny and went up to three pence during the late twenties. A postcard was a ha'penny."

Here is Stanhope Road

Starting at Willis Road were **Speedwell Buildings**, more office accommodation as well as the Speedwell Temperance Hotel and the picture house. The Speedwell Hotel was built in 1890 with 84 bedrooms. The picture house was opened on the 16th of December 1913 by Alderman Sir George Couzens K.L.H. The first day's receipts were divided between Portsmouth Care Fund and the Evening News Boot Fund. A fine orchestra accompanied silent films. The hotel closed in 1920 and the cinema extended to include a tea gallery. The cinema closed in 1929 and became a funfair. The site was redeveloped in the thirties for office and shop use.

Then came **Central Buildings**. Liptons the tea merchants were here as was the **Singer Sewing Machine Co.**

89 was **Central Chambers** with various solicitors and the London & Provincial Bank Limited on the ground floor.

91 **Wilts & Dorset Bank Ltd.** Later Lloyds bank and then the Halifax Building Society.

93 On the corner with Edinburgh Road was the **Central Hotel** which was destroyed in the air raid of 1941.

> "It was a big hotel, the biggest in Portsmouth and had about 100 rooms. It absolutely dominated the curve of the road. It was about seven stories high and was used mainly by commercial travellers."

Here is Edinburgh Road

Round the corner in Edinburgh Road was the **Coliseum**, formerly the Empire. It opened in 1891 and was demolished in 1958 and Sainsbury's supermarket built on the site.

> "It was 4d in the Gods and a shilling for a booked seat in the front row of the circle. In the interval you could go to the bar where a pint of beer was 4d and so was a packet of 10 cigarettes."

> "People used to queue up outside for the two houses and while we were queuing up there were all sorts of acts and buskers; even little kids would do a song and dance act. One fellow sold Paregoric sweets 'Cough No More' sweets at a penny or tuppence a bag. One night there was an escapologist and he offered to let anyone tie him up with rope and he guaranteed to escape in two minutes. Some sailors tied him up and he couldn't get out and we all went in and left him on the pavement."

On the other side of Edinburgh Road was an entrance to the Arcade on the corner of which was the Swiss Cafe.

> "My parents came to Portsmouth from Switzerland in 1893 and brought continental cooking to the city. My father had a restaurant opposite the end of Arundel Street and then moved in 1908 and opened the

Continental Cafe near the Theatre Royal. His brother had his restaurant on the corner of the Arcade called the Swiss Cafe. We have a picture of them standing outside with old-fashioned waiters wearing the long Paris type aprons."

95-97 On the other corner of Edinburgh Road was **Barclays Bank Ltd.**

99 **The Landport Arms**, listed here from 1844, in Union Road, until 1940 when it was destroyed in the war along with many other properties in the area.

101 **W.G.Chapman,** watchmaker, later Ingersoll Watch Co. Ltd.

103 **Ellis Bros & Co. Ltd.**, tailors.

105 **Maypole Dairy Co. Ltd.**, butter merchants.

> "We used to go there. We were poor and when we had company mother used to say "Go down the Maypole and get half a pound of margarine and see that they print it!" They used to pat it up with butter pats and stamp a picture on top, a cow I think."

107 **George Dean**, tailor. Earlier this had been from 1859 to 1882 the Norfolk Arms, later becoming an off license. Next door at 105 in the 1863 directory only was The Drum.

109-113 **Landport Drapery Bazaar**, later moved along a few doors.

111 Was previously the Swiss Cafe.

115 **Lloyds Bank Ltd**, previously Capital & Counties Bank.

Here is the Arcade

The cinema inside the arcade, The Arcade Picture Palace, opened in November 1911. The proprietor was J.W.Mills. It was bombed on the 10th of January 1941, although the Arcade itself survived into the early fifties.

> "This was one of the finest shopping places in Portsmouth. It was covered with a lovely glass roof and the sun pouring through. There were shops on both sides; flowershops, toyshops, clothes and ribbons, photographs, service badges and buttons. When it rained they did a good trade and many people walked through to Victoria Park. It was destroyed by bombs in 1941, what a pity it wasn't built back again after the war."

"Just along inside the Arcade was a shop run by an Italian lady and her daughter. You paid a penny to play their machines. They had a bird cage you put a penny in to make the bird sing; I saw one just like it on the 'Going for a Song' programme. She also told fortunes."

"There was a fine cinema inside the Arcade, it was called the flea pit. We used to call it the bug hutch and when you came out you felt a bit itchy. A load of tramps used to get in there. It was only thruppence in the afternoon and if you were out of work and looking for somewhere to sit in the warm...well. The first 7 or 8 rows of seats were just wooden benches, then the dearer seats were chairs, with all the springs sticking up. It was only a small cinema and you came in at the side of the screen."

117 Arcade Chambers, Robert Mason, costumier.

Later 117-119 became **Landport Drapery Bazaar** house furnishers.

121-125 F.W.Woolworth & Co. Ltd., earlier **Barnes & Seager Ltd**, wallpaper merchants, **Maynards Ltd.**, confectioners and **W.Hartley & Co.**, Naval and Civilian tailors.

"Everything was 3d or 6d; a galvanised bath twenty inches long, for washing clothes or babies in was 6d."

"You went in there for things like writing books, and pens and pencils, thread and ribbon, and haberdashery type goods. Every Woolies you went in had the same; wooden floors, wooden counters with glass dividers and everything piled in the compartments with the cream and red labels in their metal holders. Cheap china was another thing, you could buy a piece at a time until you had a set."

"Every so often they would have a bargain weekend where they would sell large buckets, enamel bowls....I've heard it said they cost the shop sevenpence ha'penny and they used to sell them for sixpence. They would have a queue outside waiting for these special bargains and of course when you went in you bought other things as well, so all in all it proved profitable to them."

131-137 Ross and Holman, house furnishers, later to become **True-Form Boot Co.** and **Boots** the chemist.

> "In those days you could buy a bedroom suite for about £20 and an average dining room suite was about £17 - £20. Most people had their stuff on the slate, you could buy secondhand but people would go into debt to have new."

139 Currys Cycle Co., cycle manufacturers.

141 H.Samuel Ltd., jewellers.

143 Domestic Bazaar Co. Ltd. A lot earlier from 1851 until 1863 it was a beer retailer only named in the 1863 directory, the Bull's Head.

145 G.Bateman & Co. Ltd., Opticians.

> "Lots of people in those days went to Woolworth for their glasses. I remember my Gran going there to buy a pair. You picked up the different pairs and there was a test card and you just tried them until you could read the print and that was the pair you bought for sixpence. They were steel rims and very plain but they were very good and helped lots of people."

147 W.Welch, bookshop

> "I was an engineering apprentice and that was the only bookshop in Portsmouth which dealt with the trades. It was a most superior bookshop and the books would be bought by Naval Officers and so on. The principal book for us was 'Southerns Marine Steam Turbines' and that was on sale for about £5 a time. We were earning about 7/6d and our eyes would goggle at the books in there; we had to go to the library to borrow our books. Two delightful ladies ran it; one I can see now, a rather big woman with grey hair, a most pleasant lady."

149 G.Oliver, boot maker, later the **Home and Colonial Stores Ltd.**

Behind Pickett's the jewellers was **The Classic Cinema**

The Cinenews Cinema opened on the 14th of September 1936 and sat 453 people. It showed newsreels, cartoons and general interest films. Admission was 6d downstairs and 1/- upstairs. On the 5th of July 1937 the name was changed to Classic. The cinema closed on the 6th of August 1972 and was demolished.

"In those days, on a Sunday night, everyone used to line up for the cinema, there was little else to do. The Classic was only small. It was 6d downstairs and 1/3d upstairs. If you were young and took a girl to the pictures and went out with two shillings, you were with the aristocracy. We used to buy a quarter pound box of chocolates and, to make the luxury complete, ten cigarettes."

151-153 **T.Pickett Ltd.**, jewellers. John Purser & Sons were at 181, before the two joined to become Pickett & Purser.

"He was one of the first people down that way to own a car, a large Lagonda that used to be kept just inside Crasswell Street. Everyone would go and look at it, it was quite a treat just going to see it."

155-157 **G.A.Dunn & Co. Ltd.**, the Hatters. Previously **Lennards Ltd.** a boot makers. On the corner of Meadow Street, one of the few surviving pre-war shops in Commercial Road. (Demolished in 1989) Always a high class shop known for their six shilling bowlers.

Here is Meadow Street.

159 **S.R. & T.Clegg**, brush and seed merchants. Later with 161 to become **Montague Burton Ltd.**, tailors.

161 **Perfect & Co.**, chemists

"It was very small and in the doorway was a basket where you could weigh the baby, a clean cloth in the basket and you could weigh the baby for a penny."

163 **Brandons Ltd.**, progressive tailors.

169-171 **The Penny Bazaar** (1908-1916), later 163-173 **Marks and Spencers**

"My what a wonderful shop that was. Everything seemed to be in small baskets, round baskets and you went in and took out the stuff you wanted and took it to the girl. It was all 1d or 3d or thereabouts."

173 **Albert Clapham**, cake shop & confectioner.

"It was different from today; it was kind of greasy and steamy like some seaside shops are. I remember the wasps in there because of the sweet stuff. They had a live cockatoo in there on a perch and now and then some kid would squawk at him and he would squawk back, they used to take a delight in upsetting him."

175 **John Vokes**, china and glass dealer.

> "Vokes was chock-a-block with china of all sorts, windows full of chambers. Outside they had all china teapots on a long board, all wired and nailed so they couldn't be stolen. There was straw everywhere too."

> "Vokes was a long narrow shop. You could buy a cup and saucer for 3d or a teaset for three shillings. All their glass and china were of excellent make and value."

177-179 **Leonard Bros**, tailors.

181 **John Purser & Sons Ltd.**, jewellers.

183 **J & G.H.Roe Ltd.**, boot makers.

185 **Collett & Co.**, Wine and Spirit merchants.

187-189 **Gordon Lyall**, tailor.

191 **Pearks' Dairies Ltd.**

> "This particular shop specialised in butter and they would have big pats of butter, kept cool in water. You could have any sort of butter, half a pound, a quarter, two ounces and they would knock it about and give you any shape. They had various moulds and they would make it look real tempting."

193 **Carlton Shoe Co.**

195 **Fleming, Reid & Co. Ltd.**, Scotch wool stores.

Here was an alleyway next to **Samuels** the jewellers.

> "There was a little alleyway and at the end of it was the Nags Head at number 199A. There was a cast iron toilet there where they used to play pitch and toss and they used to have a couple of boys there as look out. They'd give them 2d to look out and give them the word if the police came."

The Nag's Head, listed in the trade directories from 1880 to 1940 as a beer retailer, only named in the 1887 directory. It was a Long's house.

> "The Nags Head was kept for a number of years by a man named Bungy Pharoah. He was very popular and would treat all his customers

like they were all his family. On Sunday morning he would put up pressed beef, pickled onions, cheese ... and it was all help yourself."

"At the Nags Head the manager used to leave a bottle of beer for the night-duty policeman in the 1930s who was responsible for the immediate area. The system collapsed in about 1937 when someone drank the beer and replaced it with urine!"

197-199 **H.Samuel Ltd.**, jewellers.

Here was Lower Church Path, on the corner of which was **Coleman** the fruiterer and on the opposite corner was **Harveys** the tobacconist.

"The policeman who did point duty outside used to hang his cape up in there. One well known policeman down there was called 'chesty' - a big bloke. Mind, you had to have big policeman in those days with the types that got round that way."

201 **Garcia Bros**, The Chocolate King.

"They were originally street traders and took up sweet selling straight from the suppliers or manufacturers. On Friday you had all the Dockyardmen coming up to buy sweeties for their children. They'd go home with paregoric boiled sweets, coconut ice, boiled fishes, peanut brittle and, of course, chocolate. It was 6d a pound and came in big slabs they broke up with a thing like a scissor with a very sharp bit on the end."

Here is Charlotte Street

On the other corner of which at 203 was the **Monarch or Monarch Tavern.** Listed here from 1863 to 1940. Originally it was a Brown's of Charlotte Street house. In 1962 the Crown from opposite transferred to the site and survived a few more years to 1976. It is now a jewellers shop.

205 **Parkers (Portsmouth) Ltd.**, butchers.

207 **Fuller's Hall** and provision market opened on the 1st of October 1886. The entrances were 207 Commercial Road and 4-6 Charlotte Street. The proprietor was Henry Fuller. By 1896 the hall was known as St. James Hall. Mr Frank Pearce had taken over by 1902 and it was known as St. James Concert and Variety Hall. From 1912 the entrance was from Charlotte Street only. The hall was also known as Jury's Picture Palace from 1913-1917 and

from 1918 on as just St. James Hall. In 1927 it became the St. James Temperance Billiards Club and it closed in 1933. The Commercial Road part became the **Halford Cycle Co. Ltd.**

209 **G & G Curtis Ltd.**, corn chandler.

> "Curtis had a very large shop for corn and dog biscuits and all sorts; sackfuls all over the place. They used to loan horses out to the Dockyard and they were kept in Commercial Place and led out to the Dockyard every morning and back at night. Quite a procession to watch."

> "The reason why there were so many corn chandlers is because of the number of horses in the period, which also accounts for the number of public houses. It didn't matter then about drinking and driving a horse as it does today when you're drinking and driving a motor car."

211 **N.S.Harvey & Co.**, tobacconists.

213-215 **David Greig Ltd.**, Grocer. Formerly Hutchinsons the grocer.

> "I can just remember Hutchinsons, you used to purchase bacon one side and your cheese the other. You bought what you wanted and took your money to the centre to the cashier. You brought your half the bill back and when you got back it would be all nicely wrapped up for you."

> "Everything in those days was weighed and put in a cone of blue paper; cheese was cut fresh and a snippet given to you to taste. You could buy a ha'peth of piccalilli or pickled onions, a farthing's worth of vinegar or salad cream."

217 In 1911 listed as **The Gaiety Picture Saloon**, but the Gaiety Picture Palace built by John Lay was opened on the 13th of September 1912. The owner was William Keast a showman and former Klondyke goldminer. The cinema had wooden seats for about 150 people, admission was a penny or twopence. The cinema closed in 1917 and became Keast's gramophone shop. Currys now occupy the site.

219-223 **George Couzens & Son**, ironmongers. Later taken over by Jay's the furnishers.

> "Couzens sold kettles, pots and pans, nails and tacks, and so forth. Saucepans were usually cast iron and if they were leaking you went to

21

the ironmonger and bought a pot-mender and repaired it yourself. A pot-mender was two circles of steel with a screw and you enlarged the hole in the pot, put one circle each side of the pot and screwed it up tight. Aluminium didn't come in until later."

225 **Weston Burt**, draper.

"A double-fronted shop selling haberdashery and ladies underwear."

227 **The Suffolk Arms**. Established in 1857 it was rebuilt in 1907 and again partially in 1957. It had its own brewery and was renamed Martha's after one of its licensees, Martha Kingsbury. She was the wife of the well known cyclist.

"Each pub was noted for different things and each had its own sort of customer. Martha's was where naval personnel went; stokers and so on, everyone but ERA's. They used the pub on the corner of Station Street, Judds."

"The Suffolk Arms was very popular. It was a free house and usually known as Martha's. I've heard it said that all over the world sailors would say 'See you in Martha's'. It was on the corner and I've heard it called Pudding Alley, because it led to Pye Street."

In fact the pub stood on the corner of *Providence Path* not very aptly named since Baker's the pawnbrokers was on the corner.

229-231 **Baker & Co.**, pawnbrokers.

"Well known, well used and very, very useful."

233 **Hampshire Furnishing Co.**

235-237 **Stephen Shoebridge**, draper.

239 **Albert Fielder**, watchmaker later he became an opticians.

241 **William Williams**, Post Office.

"Williams was not a very big shop but they had fancy goods and they always had the wooden horses for the kiddies, with a round body and a flat head, for two or three shillings. They had buckets and spades and things like that so that when people went across to draw their money and had their kiddies with them, they were sure of buying them a bucket or something."

Here is Thomas Street

On the other corner of Thomas Street at 243-255 was **McIlroys Ltd**, drapers.

> "McIlroys was a marvellous shop, they did more trade than Landports. It was bombed in the war. My mother and various people we knew bought their hats there. You bought the frame and then you had it covered with ostrich feathers or whatever else you wanted."

257-259 **The Newtown Tavern.** Listed as a brewer and beer retailer from 1827 to 1886, the pub being named in the 1874 directory. The pub was rebuilt in 1902 to the designs of local architect A.E.Cogswell and survived until the 1941 bombing. The Anderson family were the brewers until the brewery and tied house became part of Gales of Horndean.

261 **George Kinson**, auctioneer, house, land and estate agents. Listed in 1859 as a beer retailer and from 1863 to 1865 as the Commercial Arms, it was owned by Anderson and may have moved to 297.

263 **W.Parnell**, umbrella maker.

> "That's another thing you had repaired. People are so well off nowadays that they don't realise how you had to be careful with things then. If you had a tear or bit of wear in an umbrella then you took it to have it mended."

265 **Farmer Shoe Co.**

267 **Harry Thelwall**, outfitter.

269-271 **Maxim Machine Co.**, domestic machine dealers.

273-275 **John Bright (Outfitters) Ltd.**, tailors.

At one time 275 was **Sevier**, Hat shop.

> "In those days everybody wore a hat. Men wore cloth caps and bowlers for best, or boaters in the summer. Women wore a hat of some kind all the time. You just didn't go out without a hat on, it would have been like going out with no clothes on."

277 **Albert Young**, chemist.

279 **William Lock**, wholesale fruiterer.

281 **William Allies**, confectioner.

283 **Woods Stores**, greengrocers.

285 **F.Lawrence**, music seller.

> "It was a musty old place. I remember there was always one sheet of music in the windows; it was called 'Fire, Fire, Fire' with a picture on the cover of a large fire going in a big house and the fire engine drawn by about six horses with steam coming out of their nostrils, rushing along. It seems to stick in my memory well."

287 **Charles Worsfold**, watch maker.

289 **Worlds Stores Ltd.**, grocers.

291 **Arthur Fletcher**, confectioner.

293 **W.L.Pinker Ltd.**, wholesale fruiterer and florist.

295 **George Hooper**, hair dresser.

297 **Commercial Arms**, listed as a beer retailer from 1874 until 1940 and only named in the 1887 directory.

299 **Masonic Arms**, named from 1863 to 1887, but only listed as a beer retailer from then until 1940. It was originally an Anderson's house.

301 **John Brown**, confectioner.

303 **Sotnik & Levison**, dealers in government stores. Later **Premier Service**, dyeing and cleaning specialists.

305 **Arthur Bullimore**, dining rooms.

> "Largely speaking, working people didn't eat out but single men, in their affluence, might go out and enjoy it. You would dress up a bit and go out in the evening for a roast, or a chop, or something like that. In the ordinary home you probably wouldn't have your meal laid out with the cutlery and so on and the up and coming generation began to learn the technique and to take it all in their stride."

307 **Paver & Son**, butchers. Later George Cooper.

309 **E.J.Stone**, outfitter.

311 **Locke Bros**, scale makers.

311a **Alfred Fehrenbach**, wholesale fruiterer.

313 **The Hants Estate Agency**

315 Royal Portsmouth Hospital. The foundation stone was laid by Prince Albert in 1847. The hospital was demolished in 1971.

The entrance to the **Royal Hospital** was a gateway built as a memorial to the dead in the First World War from the hospital. It was pulled down in August 1969 when the road was widened. It was sadly missed, but not as keenly as the hospital itself.

"The Royal was in easy reach of everybody and near the Dockyard. Now that it's shut it is a great loss to the local people. In the thirties working men paid 3d a week from their wages so that a man and his family could all have hospital treatment and entry to the hospital free. This was very good and lasted right up to just after the war when the Government took over all the hospitals and everyone was given free treatment and care."

"When I was about twelve, I was the paper delivery boy in the Royal; you couldn't take regular orders because of the floating population. During the football season I had to take the Mails and at the end of the 26/27 season Portsmouth's promotion to the first division depended on the last game on a Saturday, against Preston North End. When I took round the Mails everyone was so excited they would give me sixpence and say 'That's alright son, keep the change.' So it was right round the hospital. When I got back and sorted out the money, I had more money in tips than I had to hand over."

"You used to be able to buy dripping from the Royal and the word went round us kids that the dripping came out of the arms and legs they had cut off. Same with the soup kitchen at All Saints Church opposite, all the kids used to say the arms and legs were in there."

317 The Mile End Tavern next to the entrance to the Royal Hospital. One of the older houses of the area listed as far back as 1823 at Newtown, later at Eden Row. It was a Pike's house.

"I played whist in there; I used to represent the Mile End Tavern and I won a gold medal when we won the championship of the whist league. All the horses for the market used to be kept at that tavern."

321 Frederick Ward, wholesale fruit merchant.

323-325 **Gleeson & Talbot** later **Gleeson & Powell**, physicians and surgeons. The houses were demolished in 1941.

> "Dr Olaf Gleeson was one of the first Labour members on Portsmouth Council and was one of the finest men to poor people. He would say 'You pay me a penny or tuppence when you can' and he never by-passed anyone."

Here is Fitzherbert Street.

327 **Way & Westby**, physicians and surgeons.

329 **Walter Barwick**, tobacconist.

331 **George Hill**, confectioner.

333-337 **Doudney & Co. Ltd.**, Soap Works.

> "It used to smell something awful. They were very well known for their high class soaps made with poultry fats. There were so many slaughterhouses in Portsmouth, and poultry shops, they would take the fats there; goose fat, chicken fat or whatever fats they had and it was all made into high class soaps."

> "I've been in there for maggots when we were going fishing over the hill. They were from the fat and it was really revolting."

The **Savoy Cinema** was later built on the site. It opened in the 17th of July 1937 by Lord & Lady Mayoress F.J.Spickernell. The opening film was 'That Girl From Paris' and the Compton Wonder Organ was played by Reginald Porter-Brown. It later became the ABC and in 1986 a Cannon cinema. The organ was removed to Devonshire Avenue Baptist Church in 1966.

345 **Hills & Son**, potato merchants.

347 **E.Lakeman**, tailor.

349 **S.P.Boot Co.**, boot factors.

351 **George Stent**, clothier.

353 **Mason & Co.**, potato merchants.

355 **G.Pearce & Son**, wholesale fruiterers.

357 **Hooper, Collet & Wood**, printers and bookbinders.

359 **J.Welch & Sons**, photographic publishers.

Joseph Welch is listed as a photographer in the 1875 trade directory at 213 Commercial Road. In 1887 the firm had become Welch Bros. In 1898 Joseph Welch & Sons are listed at Cheapside in Lake Road as Photographic Publishers. They returned to Commercial Road remaining until 1936. They published a large range of local postcards, many featuring members of the family amongst the crowds. The glass plates on which the photographs were taken were sadly destroyed in the war.

365 **Green & Green**, surgeons.

367 **Oldfield Brothers**, mineral water manufacturers. Behind which was Hostler's sweet factory, this later moved to Cosham Street.

> "Which gave off a beautiful smell."

> "My sister left school and went to work there at fourteen years of age. She was there a fortnight and she caught her hand in one of the machines. They had to rush her to the Royal and to this day she has the marks. It was a machine for cutting sweets and she had to feed in the mixture. There was no guard and she caught her hand; she was lucky she didn't lose all her fingers."

369 **Frederick Saddon**, tobacconist.

371 **The Robin Hood**, listed from 1863 to 1953 as Robin Hood, or Robin Hood Tavern. In early days had its own brewery.

Here is Pitt Street with the recreation ground.

> "During the war the stables where the Dockyard horses were kept, in Commercial Place, were set on fire and my husband went to help. He told them to let them go free, horses always find their own safety. Next day they were all found up in Pitt Street Rec. apparently the gate was left open during the blitzes for an open space for emergencies."

373 **J.B.Ward & Sons**, bakers.

375 **Mile End Tavern**. Listed from 1865 to 1977 when it was demolished and rebuilt becoming the Oliver Twist. It was a Gale's house.

377 **Harry Simpson**, Mile End Dairy.

Mile End was the northern end of the wholesale vegetable market.

"Three mornings a week my husband was in Commercial Road market at 4a.m. The growers used to bring in their things by horse and cart and the traders were there to buy. The market was from the Royal Hospital to Charlotte Street. A girl from the Salvation Army Hostel in Villiers Road used to come with a truck and the growers used to give her vegetables; I've seen that truck loaded high."

"The market was on three days a week. It was over by about 8.30am and they came home at about five. They used to come from as far as Bosham, Chichester and so on. The small greengrocers used to come to get their produce and any individual could go along too as long as he bought at least a shillingsworth. A shillingsworth of mixed vegetables in those days was a small sackfull; potatoes, carrots, cabbage, onions, leeks, in season. Plenty of unemployed people and those whose money was a bit tight, that shillingsworth would last them all week."

"My brother in law used to stand near the Mile End Dairy with his store of produce which he used to bring from his small holding at Soberton, leaving at 4am and collecting from others in his van. Some traders used to get him to deliver stuff once they had bought it."

389 Commercial Road Baptist Chapel. The site was bought in 1884 from Mr Palmer for £1,600 by Clarence Street Baptist Church whose members desired a more prominent position. The foundation stones were laid on the 8th of October 1884. The architect was Mr Edward Wright of Southend and the builder Mr Croad of Portsea. The church opened on the 16th of March 1885 and remained in use until 1920 when the congregation moved again this time to Tangier Road. The building was used from 1923 until 1981 by the Municipal College and the Highbury Technical College. In 1990 it was being used as an art gallery. Behind it was a Smith's Crisps factory which gave off a horrible greasy smell.

Here is Mill Lane, which used to lead down to the Union Mill and bakehouse. The mill being both wind and steam driven.

391 Dr Maybury, jun.

393 Charles Dickens Birthplace Museum

"I remember at the age of ten we had the Tale of Two Cities as a class reading book. I went to Dicken's house out of curiosity because it was mentioned, it was free then. One of the questions in the exam was

'Write a list of all the hard words you have learned' and feeling I had to put down something I put down missure and I got three stokes of the cane."

397 The Old Well House still has a well in the garden.

401 **Dr Maybury**, sen. The first Doctor Maybury lived here when it was still a large country house in its own grounds. His son was the second Doctor Maybury.

"He was a famous man. He was very imposing, with mutton chop whiskers, a real gentleman. He used to go round in a horse and trap and later a lovely old chauffeur driven car; a Swift, with brass headlamps, wearing a Billy Cock hat."

403 **George Donaldson**, chemist.

405 **Smiths Potato Crisps** later **John Buttigieg**, confectioner.

Here is Herbert Street

On the corner was **Winchester College Mission High School** (1907-1916), run by the Rev. Dolling, who built the new St. Agatha Church. Rev. Dolling lived in the mission headquarters in Clarence Street where he and his sister kept open house for the poor, the needy and the homeless.

407 **Beale, Dennis & Milham**, house agents.

409 **McKinlay & Co. Ltd.**, engineers.

411 **Frank Howell**, stationer, post office and undertaker.

413 **James Paxman**, jeweller.

415 **Singer Sewing Machine Co. Ltd.**

417 **Home & Colonial Stores Ltd.**

419 **Robert Marshall**, grocer.

Here is Regent Street

"The houses in Regent Street had no bathrooms, just outside toilets. We used to warm water for a bath in the copper there was no electricity or gas, just a kitchen range. There was no back garden just a backyard backing out onto the yards of Herbert Street."

"I used to fetch Grandfather's beer in a jug from the pub at the corner of Regent Street and his tobacco, price elevenpence ha'penny an ounce, from Barretts tobacco shop at the top of Regent Street."

423 **Edwin Barrett**, tobacconist.

425 **The Osborne Hotel**, the Osborne Tavern from 1863 to 1896, Hotel from 1897 to 1970 when it was closed and demolished. It was another of Lush's houses.

Here is Prospect Road

427 **The Sailors Return**, listed from 1863 to 1973 when it was demolished. It was a George Peters house becoming Ind Coope. It was a small white pub with a corrugated iron roof and had a sign which read:

> *This sign hangs high*
> *and hinders none*
> *Refreshment take*
> *and then jog on.*

429 **John Adams**, butcher. Later Gassers.

"Everyone was busy then, butchers and slaughtermen cleaning out until late at night. Roast Pork was 6d a quarter, pigs feet a ha'penny, a tasty knuckle with plenty of meat tuppence, pork pie tuppence ha'penny. Chitterlings cleaned and salted, my dad stayed up all night putting them in brine after they were plaited. Mawl and corned leg, brisket of beef to be pressed, all in huge copper in the backyard, and the mooing of the cows waiting to be slaughtered."

"One pennyworth of mixed vegetables was enough to make a stew for six people, and then to the butchers to get a tuppenny ha'penny breast of lamb or four penn'eth of beef cuttings with kidneys. With a penn'eth of suet for the dumplings, or to make a nice crust for a steak and kidney pudding ample for eight people."

431 **William Freeborn**, fruiterer.

433 **Dark & Davey**, tobacconist.

435 **Miss Browne**, fancy draper.

437 **Bertram Coombs**, corn dealer.

The Sailor's Return

439 **William Ritson**, boot maker.

441 **Frank Elliot**, hairdresser.

443 **Urry & Tee**, pawnbrokers.

Here was Wolfe Road.

445-447 **Ben Grubb & Elliot**, general dealers.

449 **Our Dumb Friends League** cats and dogs shelter.

McKinlay & Co. Ltd, Mile End Works.

451 **Bailey & Whites Ltd.**, timber and slate importers & joinery manufacturers.

> "As a boy, apprenticed carpenter, I pushed the handcart to Bailey & Whites, where I met the governor who arrived in style in his Morris 8. He would give the ganger 6d to pick out the best timbers; without too many knots, not too much dampness and as straight as possible. Once my cart was loaded with as much as I could push I made my way back around the Dockyard walls to Union Street."

Here was Kettering Terrace

Then two private houses before *Albion Street*

459 **Alex Desbois**, house furnisher.

461 **William Whiting**, confectioner.

463 **David Mitchell**, hairdresser.

467 **Cramptons (Shipbuilders) Ltd**, Albion Shipyard. Later became **Albert Kemp**, joinery manufacturers.

469 **The Lord Nelson**, another of the early public houses. Known from 1823 to 1851 as the Nelsons Arms, becoming the Lord Nelson by 1859. It is first listed at Kingston, then Mile End. It was demolished in 1974.

Then came **Mile End Cemetery**, which opened in 1831, now the lorry park for the ferry port.

> "I remember it when all the stones had been moved to the sides and it was all grass. It was an oasis of green. I used to take my daughter there when she was a baby. I was really upset when they dug it all up to extend the docks - I even wrote to the Evening News - it was a real shame.

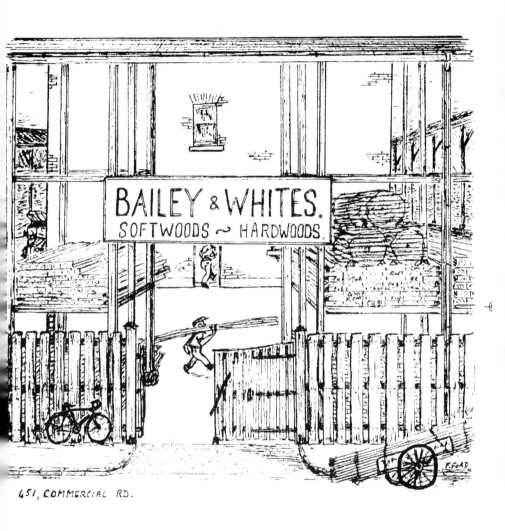

Bailey & White's

Portsea Island General Cemetery at Mile End

471A **Henry Wilkins & Sons Ltd.**, monumental masons. This later became **Pylo Motor & Cycle Depot**.

471 **Alfred Adams**, fruiterer.

473 **George Pearce**, furniture dealer.

475 **Gough & Co.**, house agents.

477 **Grubb & Elliot**, Mile End Motor Garage.

Here was Wharf Road

483 **The Hearts of Oak**. Listed as a pub from 1874 to its demolition in 1974 in the trade directories, the original house dates from 1858. It was a Bransbury's house, refronted in 1897-1900 by the local architect A.E.Cogswell for Brickwoods at a cost of £1,230. The unusual front of the building was taken down piece by piece and is stored at the museum, hopefully to be re-erected at some time in the future.

501 **Baron Products Co.**, patent medicine manufacturers. Later the **Customs & Excise & Old Age Pensions Office**.

503 **Dr.R.Weston & Dr.K.O'Sullivan**.

505 **Premier Providing Co.**, credit drapers, clothiers and furnishers.

Here is Watergate Road. Rudmore Gas Works were built in 1875 and demolished in 1977.

511 **J.R.Wood & Co. Ltd.**, coal merchants, reflecting the nearness of Rudmore Quay.

> "Rudmore was a haven of ships bringing loads of fruit, cauliflowers and fishermen for whelks, cockles, eels, flat fish and crabs. I remember one man used to bring his horse and cart, lined with fern leaves - lovely crabs 6d each, cleaned and dressed on the spot, flat fish, butterfish, scallops, oysters and lobsters straight from the pot."

513 **Donald McSweeney**, hairdresser.

515 **George Pearce**, furniture dealer.

517 **F.E.French & Son**, leather merchants.

519 **Charles Saunders**, butcher.

Hearts of Oak

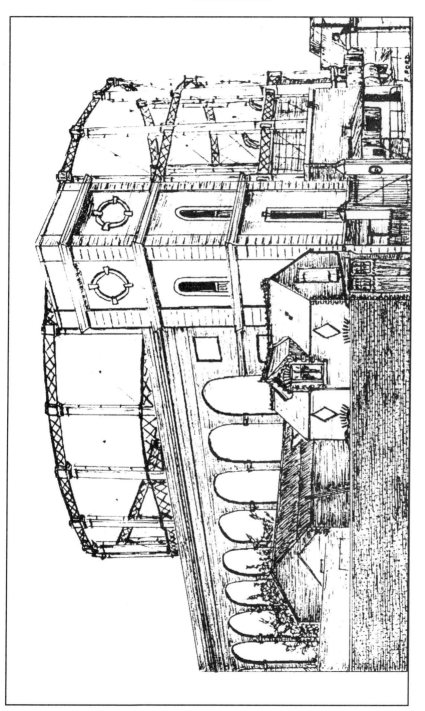

Rudmore Gas Works, Watergate Road

521 **Princess Royal**, First listed in 1863, then does not appear again until 1887. It closed in 1968 and was demolished.

523 **Alfred Jacobs**, house furnisher.

Here is Rudmore Road

525 **Frederick Franklin**, grocer.

527 **Alfred Dawson**, confectioner.

529 **C.Cooper & Sons**, butchers.

531 **Timothy White & Company Ltd.**, chemists.

533 **Bennet & Daley**, tobacconists.

535 **Dr. Josiah Blackman**, medical practitioner and medical officer for the Landport District.

Crossing the road and working our way back along the east side of Commercial Road.

598 **The Air Balloon**. Another of the early public houses of the area dating back to at least 1823. Also like the other early houses it has changed address from Kingston, to London Road before the road became Commercial Road. Its name has similarly varied, Air Balloon, Balloon and The Air Balloon. It was probably first built around the time of the first balloon ascent. It was rebuilt, in 1902 or 1905 depending which book you refer to, to the designs of local architect A.H.Bone and as we mentioned earlier is similar in style to the White Swan at the southern end of the road. It was a Bransbury's house before becoming a Brickwood's pub.

> "In about 1830 it was the last resting place of the last man punished for 'felo de se' - suicide. A young soldier from Clarence Barracks shot himself with a musket and according to statute, the body of this unfortunate young man was, in the evening of the same day taken to the highway by the Air Balloon. A grisly ceremony, a stake was driven through his heart, was performed with the constable and church warden present."

Here is Garfield Road

On the other corner was **Flying Bull Lane School**, built in 1874.

596 **E.Wakeford**, musical dealer.

594 **Mrs Sarah Locke**, tea rooms. Later used by **Locke Bros** as an extension to the shop at 588.

592 **Miss Pitt**, post office.

590 **William Black**, hairdresser.

588 **Locke & Evans**, furniture dealers.

578 **Miss Rose Ralph**, ladies' school.

570 **George Andrews**, watchmaker.

564 **Edward Burchell**, tobacconist.

Here is Elm Road

540 **Miss Rose**, The Carlton, confectionery

536 **The Royal Naval Firemans Society**

534 **Portsmouth Machine Co.**

528 **Clipper Schooner**, Listed as a beer retailer from 1859 until 1934. It was named The Schooner in the 1863 directory and Clipper Schooner in the 1887 directory. It was a Palmer's house.

518 **John Barleycorn**, listed as a beer retailer from 1874, named in the 1882 directory, it survived until 1973 when it was demolished and was a Brickwood's house.

514 **W.T.Harris & Son**, cycle agents.

508 **Mrs Graham**, credit draper.

486 **Farlington Laundry**, receiving office.

474 **The Royal Naval Lodge of Oddfellows** (Manchester Unity)

Here is Grafton Street

472 **The Market House Tavern** on the corner of Grafton Street listed in the directories from 1852 it was a Pike Spicer house.

Here was Emanuel Street

464 **Leaver & Co.**, basket makers.

462 **Angus Jamieson**, fishmonger.

460 **Mrs Bullingham**, milliner.

458 **Mrs Ethel Waller**, confectioner.

Here was Brompton Road

and a few doors along Brompton Passage

444 **Price Brothers**, bakers.

440 **William Peace,** furniture dealer.

Here was Sultan Road

438 **Arthur Savage**, fried fish shop.

436 **W.Pink & Sons Ltd.**, fruiterers and grocers, later Harrow Stores, outfitters.

432-434 **Hart & Wheeler**, tailors and outfitters.

Here were Winchester Buildings

428 **Arthur Roberts**, physician & surgeon.

424 **Mrs F.Limburn**, confectioner.

422 **William Hardy**, pork butcher. Later became **William Stephens**.

420 **Harry Beale**, cycle agent. Later became a stationers and Post Office.

418 **Mrs J.Wait**, fruiterer.

416 **Joseph Buttigieg**, confectioner who moved to 405. The premises here becoming **Albert Cooper**, butcher.

Here was Prince's Street

412 **Harold Churchill**, newsagent.

410 **La Rooy**, hairdresser.

408 **Thompson & Sons**, motor engineers.

402-404 **St Mary's Convent (Helpers of the Holy Souls)**. The order opened on the 16th of July 1913. It closed in 1978.

400 **George Griffiths**, watch maker.

398 **William Stoneham**, boot maker.

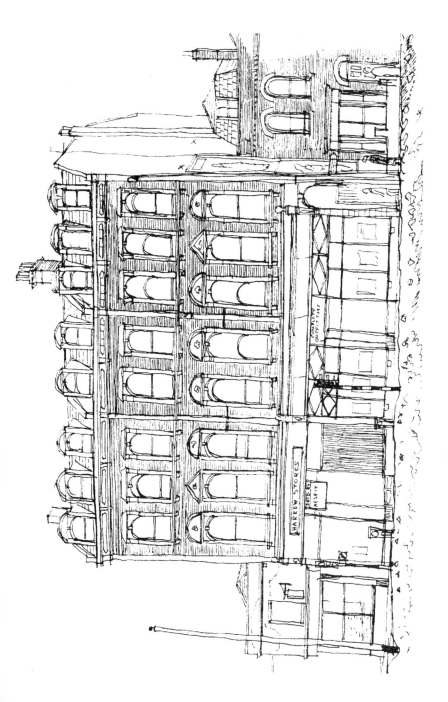

Old Harrow Stores, Commercial Road

Here was Victoria Street

388 **George Oliver**, boys' school, Mile End School. Built in the 1850's the school closed in 1986 and has since been converted into flats.

Before the war their fees were 6 guineas a term for daily boys and 50 guineas for boarders, more if over 12. Extras included 2 guineas a term for Latin, 3 for shorthand and typing, and 2 for book-keeping, chemistry or physics.

386 **The White Lion**, listed in the trade directories from 1863 until 1969. It was earlier the White Lion Brewery advertised for sale in the 1855 Hampshire Telegraph.

Here was Providence Place.

382-384 On the opposite corner was **Papps & Son**, piano factory.

Here was All Saints View

376-378 **Lillie & Co.**, timber yard

Here was Norfolk Place

358a **Mile End Cycle & Radio Co.**

358 **Frederick McMahon**, dentist.

Here was Mile End Place

356 **Patrick McGinn**, physician & surgeon.

348 **W.L.Pinker Ltd.**, potato merchants.

344 **Gospel Assembly Room**

From 1881 to 1940 was a Gospel Mission Hall. It then became a builders store until 1967. Ben Grubb took the premises over in 1971 and continued the well known surplus stores. The rear and south walls still revealed the Gospel Hall origins of the building. It was demolished in 1982.

342 **The Countryhouse**, First listed in the trade directories in 1865, it was a Blake's of Gosport house. It was demolished in 1982.

Here is All Saints Road and Church Street

All Saints Church

The foundation stone was laid by the Rev. Henville on the 24th of June 1825. The building design is attributed to the Owen family but there is some doubt as to whether it was the father, Jacob, or the son, Thomas. The church was consecrated on the 15th of April 1828 by the Bishop of Winchester and had cost £13,000. The chancel was added in 1877 at a cost of a further £8,000, again there is some discrepancy, this time Sir Gilbert Scott or his son John Oldrich Scott. A.E.Cogswell the local architect was responsible for the restoration of 1913. In 1940 the church suffered bomb damage, but was restored during the period 1950-1955. In 1975 the interior was remodelled to the designs of Thomas Makins to suit modern requirements at a cost of £100,000.

338-340 **Mrs Haines**, wardrobe dealer. Later became Beaumonts.

336 **William Woodham**, credit draper.

334a **New Inn**, listed as a beer retailer from 1871. First named in the 1887 directory. The site had been a brewery from 1865 until a fire burnt down the brewery and tap in 1871. Later it suffered war damage and was refronted. In 1987 it was renamed The Royal after the old Royal Hospital that used to stand opposite, where the new Sainsburys supermarket and car park are now.

Here is All Saints Street

326-334 **Warrington Woven Wire Company**, better known as Slumberland Beds, they later moved to Penny Street.

324 **Watson & Ockenden**, fruit merchants.

322 **Fred Vince**, fruiterer.

318-320 **E.Cook & Son**, fruit and potato merchants.

316 **E.Hill & Son**, potato merchants.

314 **Alfred Smith**, motor engineer.

312 **Challen, Clarke & Co.**, coal merchants.

308-310 **Hancock & Son**, china and glass merchants. Later **Barnes & Seager Ltd.**, wall paper, varnish and colour merchants.

> "They had all the paints and distempers and it was afterwards called Barnes and Seagers. One of the big adverts in the window was for Halls paints where two men were carrying a board with 'Use Halls

43

Paints for All Work' on. You used to see them by the side of the railway too - life sized. It went up in smoke in about 1936/1937.

306 **Mrs Wait**, dressmaker.

304 **Mrs E.Triggs**, confectioner.

298a-302 **William Keast**, gramophone, pram & mangle dealer.

"The thing I remember about that was the life sized dog looking down the horn of a gramophone and saying 'His Masters Voice'."

"My aunt used to work for Keast's. He used to have a gold mine in the garden of the shop and he used to charge people to go over. People used to pay because the original Keast was one of the original '49'ers, an actual goldminer."

298 **Augustus Knipe**, confectioner.

296 **Alfred Lodge**, dining rooms.

294 **Shepherd & Sons**, railway and forwarding agents.

292 **H.T.Goddard & Co.**, wholesale egg and butter importers.

292-294 In 1867 was the **Britannia Music Hall**. It was used as a Sailor's Rest by Dame Agnes Weston from 1878-1882, after a short time as a Conservative Club it was used as a theatre again from 1890 to 1892 as The Gaiety Theatre of Varieties. It had a domed ceiling painted with stars. From 1897 until it burnt down in 1929 it was used as a warehouse for Goddard's.

286-288 **Worthing Fruit & Flower Co. Ltd.**

284 **Edgar Patterson & Son**, fruit merchants.

Here was Smith's Court

282 **Davidson & Son**, outfitters.

280 **W & T Avery**, scale makers and **Parnall & Sons Ltd.**, shopkeepers' sundries and utensils.

278 **Leonard Cowell**, costumier.

276 **Isaac Olswing**, wardrobe dealer.

274 **Mrs Clara Williams**, tobacconist.

272 **Fashions**, costumiers.

270 **William Baldwin**, wholesale fruit merchant. Earlier this had been the Great Britains Head pub from 1859 until 1911, although only named from 1859 onwards in the directories. It was a Brickwood's house.

Here was Staunton Street

266 **W.E.Penney & Son**, dining rooms.

> "They depended mainly on the market traders and the early morning trade - Dockyardmen going to work too. They were open very early in the morning."

Previously another pub, the Victoria, Victoria Arms or Tavern, named from 1863 until 1913, but listed as a beer retailer from 1855. It was a King's of North End house.

264 **Charles Johnson**, wholesale fruiterers.

Here was Oxford Street

260 **Christopher Wilson**, fried fish shop.

258 **Robert Glenny**, fruiterer.

These were later demolished and **City Buildings** built on the site. In these were:

> "Collets had a wine shop there. A quart bottle of wine in those days would be about two or three shillings and at Christmas time we would buy a bottle, quite a nice wine by our standards. A quart of beer or stout to take away was 10d with a penny on the bottle, whisky was 12/6d a bottle and gin about the same. In the pub a small whisky was 6d and in the pubs you could have it hot or cold; sugar on the table, sticks to stir it with all for 6d. Stout you could have warm too if you wanted, all the pubs had heaters."

Mendez

> "It was a fruit and vegetable place and what was different about it was I think they were about the last place to sell vegetables by the quart and the gallon and the pint. They all had wooden measures and they sold you potatoes by the gallon, peas by the pint and so on. It seems strange today."

5-6 **Smarts**, costumier and furrier.

> "I remember there was a fashion for Valencian hats for ladies, a flat hat like a bull fighters. They made them very attractive for ladies and everyone who was anyone bought a Valencian hat at that time."

8 **Thomas Fox**, chemist.

9 **Miss Watson**, tobacconist.

and above were **Pink's** assembly rooms. Later to become a dance hall and **Thurstons** billiard hall.

Here is Lake Road

256 **Watson**, high class confectionery, tobacco and cigarettes.

> "I don't remember the name but they were fairly high class. They used to have nice jars in the window and I remember they sold Phul Nana and Shen El Nezim cachous all to make the breath smell nice. I suppose after being in the various pubs they had quite a sale for these cachou type sweets."

> "We used to buy toffee apples for a farthing each, bigger ones with a stand of toffee were a ha'penny each; juicy tiger nuts, ha'peth of coconut loose, chocolate chewing everlasting strip."

254 **Thomas Fox**, chemist. Who moved to City Buildings.

252 **A.Andrews**, hairdresser.

250 **James Parsley**, cycle dealer. From 1863 to 1891 listed as the Cooper's Arms public house, a Brickwood's house.

246 **Emperor Of India**, listed as a beer retailer from 1855, then the London Stout House from 1863 to 1865, becoming the Prince of Wales from 1874 to 1898 and the Emperor of India from 1911 until it was demolished in 1961. A Young's house.

> "What sticks in my mind about that place was the murals, mosaic murals that were in the doorways. There was King Edward, King George and Queen Mary, all in their robes as Emperor and Empress of India. I would think if they were there today they would be priceless, although I don't suppose they were thought much of in those days."

Commercial Road 'Veg' Market

Here were Paradise Street and Commercial Place

In Commercial Place was **Bassetts.**

> "He was well known for his ham sandwiches and one of the dishes the lads used to go in for was called Help and Whiff, two slices of bread, a big plate of chips and gravy. You also had what were called the corner boys, I suppose they were all out of work. They all hung around there hoping to pick up a copper or two for a cup of coffee or tea in Bassetts."

244 On the opposite corner was **The Crown**. An early house listed from 1823 as the Crown or Crown Tavern. It is first listed at Halfway Houses, then Union Road and finally Commercial Road. It was one of Garrett's houses. When it closed in 1962 the name was transferred over the road to the corner of Charlotte Street at 203.

242 **Hipps Ltd.**, tailors.

240 **George Corbin**, boot & shoe makers.

> "They ran a club, a lot of shops in those days depended on the shilling a week clubs. I lived near there and used to buy my shoes there and they used to have a sale now and then. The normal price of mens shoes then would be 12/6d and if you went to a sale they would knock 6d off. If you wanted them on the club, they would be the full price of 12/6d."

234-238 **Porter Brothers**, later **Davidsons**, outfitters.

> "This was a large shop. They were mens' outfitters. They always had glass cases outside with ties and gloves and so on. Although they had an enormous window space as well, they always wanted to show a bit more off in glass cases which were taken out and taken in of a night. They also had big brass plates with their name on hooks along under the window and were cleaned everyday."

232 **The Duke of York**, listed as a beer retailer from 1844 to 1863 and the Lord John Russell from 1865 to 1898, becoming the Duke of York by 1899. It closed in 1953. Originally it had its own brewery.

230 **Joseph White & Co.**, oil dealers.

> "They sold putty and paint and whitening. I remember going as a boy for a ha'peth of putty. They would make paint up while you waited.

They had a colour card and a shade card and whatever you wanted they could make you. They had the linseed oil and the fullers earth and everything, all in drums. It was only a small place but they sold everything in the paint line."

228 **Alfred Dudkin** later **Mora**, photographer.

226 **George Pearce**, fruiterer.

222-224 **G & W Morton Ltd.**, boot makers.

Here was Paradise Court

220b **U.S.A. Studios**, photographers.

220 **Porter Brothers**, outfitters. Later became **Millets**.

218 **Murdoch, Murdoch & Co.**, musical instrument warehouse.

216 **Willowby Jones & Co.**, boot makers.

214 **Woolf Swick**, tailor.

212 **Bagley & Woolgar**, outfitters.

"They specialised in moleskin trousers and corduroy trousers. They were called 'Bagleys Tough'uns' and they were really hard wearing. Most people round there were connected with horses and Bagleys had the monopoly on working mens' trousers. When you bought those trousers you wore them for a couple of weeks before you could bend in them. They were very, very thick and stiff but they were hard wearing. If you bought a pair you had them for two or three years. They had a funny smell."

210 **Alfred Dudkin**, photographers.

208 **The London Tavern**, named from the 1874 directory onwards, it is listed as a beer retailer from 1859. It was a Long's house and when it closed in 1936 became a shop. It was still possible to read the name on the side under the layers of paint until the building was demolished in 1980.

"Was quite a nice public house and one of the first, I should imagine, that had a family room at the back. You could take the children on a Friday or Saturday night and have a little sing song. The person who kept it in my time was a man called George Perkins."

Here is Crasswell Street

202 **Alexander Maazzolleni**, cafe restaurant.

200 **Woolf Brothers**, tailors.

200 **Halfords**

> "That was a good shop. They had everything the cyclist would need and they were good engineers in those days. If a boy started there you could say he was on the way to being a good engineer. It sounds funny today but then cycles were much more in use than the car."

194-198 **Bishop Bros.**, boot and shoe manufacturers.

> "They had all the shoes hanging outside. They also sold clothing over the top. They ran a club and after they saw you were paying alright they would introduce you to the clothes side of it. I paid 6d a week on my first suit."

192 **Herbert Riches**, tobacconist.

190 **John Hasletine**, hosier.

186-188 **The Pelican**, listed as a beer retailer from 1844 it is called the Foresters Arms in the 1887 directory. From 1894 onwards it is shown as The Pelican. It was a Murrell's house, later Peter's. It closed in 1951.

> "They had a picture of a pelican hanging outside. I've often thought about that. In those days I don't suppose any of the children would have known what a pelican was, apart from the picture they saw there because you didn't often get taken to the zoo so you wouldn't have seen one of these strange birds."

184 **Gordon Cole**, saddlers.

> "They had a horses head outside where they would show off bridles and so on. It was a nice shop."

182 **Burtons Ltd.**, tailors

> "The fifty shilling tailor."

178-180 **G & W Morton Ltd.**, Boot and Shoe Shop

176 **C.Beaumont**, outfitters

Here is Buckingham Street in which was the cinema for the Sailors Rest and also the Soldiers, Sailors and Airmans Employment Agency.

> "In those days it was a busy thing that agency because there were plenty who would employ a pensioner from the Army or Navy because they could get them cheaper than the normal person could afford to work for."

On the opposite corner of Buckingham Street was the Sailors Rest itself.

> "They had a large restaurant on the ground floor and a sailors bar. The kitchen was underground and they had a glass pavement to let light into the kitchens and the smell that used to rise from the ventilators! I should imagine that plenty of people that were hungry could stand over there and wish they were on that side."

> "There was always a boot black boy outside the Sailors Rest. I say a boy but it might be a man. He would be kneeling there with a box you put your foot on and he would give your shoes a shine for a penny or tuppence."

Here was Chandos Street which was mainly Timothy Whites stores and the back entrances to some of the shops. It was always full of horses and carts loading up to take stuff to Timothy White's shops.

168-170 **J.Baker & Co.**, The Cloth Hall, service & civil tailors, men's and boys' outfitters, hosiers & hatters.

164-166 **F.W.Woolworth & Co. Ltd.**, fancy goods. They moved to 121-125 Commercial Road and these shops became **Burton** the tailor and **J.Lyons & Co. Ltd.**, restaurant.

164 had been from 1823 until 1914 the Bakers Arms, a Pike's public house. The cottage that housed the pub dated back to 1750.

158-162 **Timothy White & Co. Ltd.**

> "That was a great big shop. One side was a chemist and the other hardware; practically everything they sold. A lot of their stuff was called Gordon Brand. You could get soap, soda, tin-tacks, chopped wood, bundles of candles, chair-nails, chair-bonds etc. They always had baskets outside with various things in. You went to the counter and ordered what you wanted and the assistant would give you a receipt. You took it to the centre of the shop and the cashier would give

you your change and take half your receipt. There was one cashier for quite a large shop, something like the style of checkouts we have today."

154-156 **Walter Gleave**, drapers.

150-152 **George Oliver**, boot shop.

Here is Arundel Street

On the opposite corner of Arundel Street was the **Landport Drapery Bazaar**. A large department store. Destroyed by fire in 1908 and then by enemy action in 1941. It was rebuilt and later became part of the Allders group.

"It was a very, very well known shop in those days. It had arcades in the front of the shop where you could shelter from the rain. It was one of the first shops where you could walk round without being pestered with being asked what you wanted or could they help you. The basement was china and glassware all year round but about a month before Christmas it was all cleared out and completely stocked with toys. It was a real treat and everyone who had children used to take them to toyland."

"They had in there an overhead rail for taking money. It was put in a small container and they pulled a chain like a lavatory chain and away would go the bill and your cash and back it would come afterwards with your change in wrapped up. They would undo it and give it to you; it was quite a novel idea in them days."

"In about 1935 a young policeman was on duty at the junction of Arundel Street and Commercial Road, very proud of his uniform. He was watching the shop girls coming out of Landport Drapery Bazaar and proudly stopped the traffic to allow a pretty girl to come out of Arundel Street. He waved the Commercial Road traffic and coming southwards was a tram. The policeman waved for it to proceed but the driver shook his head. So he stalks to the tram and asks why he won't obey the signal. The tram driver said "I will if you get off the bloody track!" It was single track there."

136-138 **The Bedford Hotel**, Known as the Blacksmith's Arms from 1823 to 1851 and the Bedford Hotel from 1859 until 1936. Listed at Halfway Houses, Union Road, Landport Road and finally Commercial Road. It was a Pike

Spicer's house and was rebuilt in 1892 to the designs of local architect A.E.Cogswell. It was demolished.

"The Bedford was a well known hotel patronised by commercial travellers quite a lot. Round in Lower Church Path they had a large stockroom and there were always two or three men outside with large trucks who would meet the commercial travellers and take their wares round the various shops. There was a murder committed there too. The story goes that there was a young woman who was called to the door and stabbed by a naval rating."

Here was Lower Church Path

"This path led through to Upper Church Path and Church Road and eventually to St. Mary's Portsea. It was only a small path but it had wrought iron over the top with "Lower Church Path" in the wrought iron and white tiles on the side of the entrance."

130-132 **National Provincial & Union Bank of England Ltd.**

128 **Collis & Co.**, tobacconist. Had a full sized figure of a Scotsman smoking a cigar standing outside.

126 **John Maltby**, tailor.

124 **F.G.Bradbear & Co**, tobacconists.

122 **Hammonds**, confectioner.

120 **Percy Harrison**, optician. Later the **Empire Studios**

"That was a well patronised studio, they did a popular photograph three for sixpence ha'penny. Most of the lads of my age have got some kind of photograph that was taken in the Empire Studios."

118 **London Joint City & Midland Bank Ltd.**

Here is Surrey Street

"Surrey Street was a rather select street for this area and a lot of the houses did bed and breakfast."

110-114 **W.Pink & Sons Ltd.**, grocers

"That was one of the finest and most well known grocers in Portsmouth. I remember 'Mrs Gossip' in the window pouring out the Mazawatee tea. They were well known for their Christmas annual; they used to give away an annual with various prizes but you had to look all over Portsmouth in their shops to find where the prizes were hidden. It was a really good campaign and everyone looked forward to the Christmas annual at Pinks."

106-108 Albany Hotel, listed as The Dive from 1879 to 1882, Albany Hotel from 1886 to 1975 and Mighty Fine from 1976. It started as Smith's Dining Rooms/Hotel from 1855 to 1878. It was refronted in 1911 to the design of local architect A.E.Cogswell. It was an Antill's later Peter's house.

104 Salmon & Gluckstein Ltd., high class tobacconist, also known for their fine library which was 2d per week per book.

102 Criterion, listed as a beer retailer in 1859 and The Crimea from 1863 to 1874. After the rebuild of 1887 it was known as the Criterion until it was demolished in 1973. It was a Lush's house.

100 Claremont Hotel, first listed as a beer retailer in 1859, then as the Bird In Hand from 1863 to 1865, Claremont Tavern from 1874 to 1875. In 1879 it is described as the Claremont Hotel & Shades and from 1882 to 1972 as the Claremont Hotel. It was demolished in 1973 and was originally a Garrett's house.

Here is Station Street. In which was the Cremo Cake Cone Factory which introduced the cone to the English Ice Cream trade:

> "At first the trade was inclined to look askance, being used to the small pastry cornet selling at one penny or a ha'enny filled with cheap water ice from the 'Hokey-Pokey' ice-cream cart. They thought this big cornet would never sell but the Wembley Exhibition came along and they had difficulty keeping up with the demand. The Portsmouth factory employed about fourteen and also manufactured drinking straws, the wax variety of course."

98 Railway Hotel, One of the early public houses. In 1823 it was the King's Arms at Coldharbour, changing to the King's Head from 1830 to 1851. It was renamed the Railway Tavern soon after the railway first came to Portsmouth and is listed as this from 1859 until 1865, when another change was made and from 1874 to 1936 it is listed as the Railway Hotel. In 1937 it took its final name Judd's Railway Hotel after one of the licensees. It was a Spicer's house and was demolished in 1973.

96 **John Horne**, dining rooms.

94 **The Bristol**, like the nearby Railway Hotel this dates back to at least 1823 and has also had changes of name. Starting as the Carpenters Arms at Halfway Houses in 1823 until 1847 when it is at Landport Road. It became the Blacksmiths Arms by 1851, this name stuck until 1894/95 when it was renamed The Bristol until its demolition in 1973. It was a Pike's house. The lease for the original building was for 1,000 years signed in 1704.

92 **Lennox Arms**, a comparative newcomer first listed in 1863 and survived until 1973 when it was demolished.

The railway station stands virtually unchanged since it was built.

"Under the centre arch was the London Watch Company where you could watch the man doing the repairs in the window."

Passing under the railway bridge we come to the Goods station and Guildhall Square.

"In the evenings it always seemed full of people. Sailors and soldiers were always much in evidence with the local children cadging fag cards off of them. 'All the Nice Girls Love a Sailor' so the song tells us, and from what I saw in the square so did the not so nice girls! Many a Jolly Jack Tar was seen with one of theses ladies on each arm."

"Every Saturday night the 'ladies' used to get up there with their beautiful powder and their red lips and their posh hats, and they used to parade round and round. Portsmouth was full of soldiers and sailors then, we forget now what a military town Portsmouth used to be, and they were all in uniform. The thing is, the 'ladies' never caused any trouble and the police didn't arrest them because they were doing a service. There weren't any madams either, they were all free lance."

Before the Goods Station was built yet another public house used to stand in the area, the Terminus Tavern, listed from 1851 until 1865.

Here were Greetham Street and Russell Street

On the corner of Russell Street and Greetham Street was the **Sussex Hotel**, listed in the trade directories from 1851 until 1972 when it was demolished. It became a Brickwood's house with a large illuminated sign BRICKWOODS in flashing coloured lights.

Next came Russell Chambers in which was Buck's, the tools merchants.

"Buck sold tools of all sorts; bricklayers, carpenters, gardening tools, whatever the trade they sold the tools and they were very cheap. A bricklayer could buy a bricklaying trowel and a pointing trowel, good ones which would be worth about £7 today (1985), for 4/- (20p) you could buy both. A carpenter could buy a saw for about 4/11d which was pure steel and would last for years; today you would pay up to £10 or £12."

Also in Russell Chambers amongst the various legal and financial offices was the A.E.U.

"Before the war most people weren't in a union and it was a thing you had to be cagey about. It was something you kept a bit hush-hush about, same as if you were in the Labour Party. It was a long time before unions were recognised."

"People joined unions because in the thirties and before employers were paying cheap rates. They were taking people who came out of the Royal Navy with a pension and in the building and other trades they were working for less money. Immediately you belonged to the union the governor had to pay you the union rate and a lot weren't keen on doing this."

"Women didn't seem to belong to unions, that was something for the men, and for the men who were in trades or manual jobs at that. It certainly wasn't like it is today when anyone might be in a union, even vicars. Mind, the unions didn't come looking for women members and I don't think they try very hard today."

76 Royal Insurance Buildings

70-74 Motor Union Insurance Co. Ltd.

64-68 Hippodrome Theatre.

The Hippodrome was built on the site of Percy Cottage and its grounds and was opened on the 13th of May 1907 by Miss Marie Tempest. It could seat 2,000 people and had cost over £30,000. It was Portsmouth's favourite music hall, where all the stars appeared. From 1933 to 1941 films were shown on Sunday evenings. The theatre was destroyed along with many other prominent buildings by enemy action on the night of the 10th of January 1941. The site

The Hippodrome

remained undeveloped until 1986 when Hippodrome House, an office block, was built by Horton Construction to the designs of the Hedley Greentree Partnership.

> "There never were a lot of music halls in Portsmouth. They always started off with the chorus girls, like the Tiller girls, and then there would be a comedian to warm up the audience. Then a musical act. That was where I first saw Hughie Green, he was a band leader and he was only about seventeen. Larry Adler came when I was a young man ... Leslie Hutchinson ... I saw them all at the Hippodrome."

> "I remember Layton and Johnson, one played the piano the other one sang. They were coloured chaps and they were very good."

> "In the Hippodrome there was a bar at the back and you could stand up there and drink while the show was on. Occasionally you had trapeze acts that swung out over the audience ... the Harmonicas were a group of harmonica players; one of them was very tall and there was another one who was a dwarf who played a very big one. It was a good evening's entertainment there."

Here was Salem Street now re-aligned and called Dorothy Dymond Street.

62 **Chaplin & Co.**, Furniture removers and agents for the Southern Railway Co. Later it became a milk bar.

> "The Primrose Cafe that was. You went in there to buy milk shakes, milk drinks, Horlicks; stuff like that. It was always a milk bar but they don't exist anymore, not quite the same."

60 **Joseph Dickson**, tobacconist.

56-58 **Rudolph Carminati**, confectioner.

54-58 Carmos Cafe Restaurant?

54 **Linnington Brothers Ltd.**, motor engineers & body builders.

52 **Charles Brown**, restaurant. Later **Kimbell's Corner House**.

> "The great thing on Saturdays was the tea dances at Kimbells. We all used to rush to the tea dances and if you were lucky you had a pair of Joyce shoes to wear. They were the trendy shoes of the time and were flat shoes with a wedge. Nearly everybody wore suits too. If I was on

late duty I used to nip straight from the tea dance to the telephone exchange; they finished at six o'clock. If not, we used to go to the cocktail bar at the Queen's. That was the highlight of the week for me."

Here is Swan Street

50 **Yorkshire Grey**, first listed as a beer retailer from 1855 to 1859, the name first appears in the 1863 directory. Like many other public houses it was also a brewery in its early days. It was rebuilt in 1896 to the designs of local architect A.H.Bone, who was also responsible for the White Swan opposite. The style of public house was not entirely the architect's as the breweries had house themes; half timbering, ceramic glazed brickwork etc. It was rebuilt to attract theatre goers the inside had timber and ceramic clad walls with ceramic pictures. In 1981 the pub was renovated. Not that alterations to pubs are a modern idea. In 1903 the Portsmouth Times reported that the magistrates had ordered the removal of all screws and partitions on bar counters and that in future only clear glass could be used in alterations instead of figured and ground glass. The Yorkshire Grey was a George Peters & Co pub. They brewed in Kings Road and Kingston. When the pub opened it was described as having one of the finest saloon bars in Portsmouth.

"That was well known in Portsmouth as the sort of pub where if you dropped something you daren't bend down to pick it up."

46 **King & King**, auctioneers.

44 **Alexander Salvetti**, confectioner.

38-40 Offices for various solicitors and architects including George Vernon Inkpen and Bone, Sharp and Tutte.

32-36 **The Palace Cinema** was opened on the 21st of February 1921 by Mayor John Timpson on the site of Bailey's timber yard. The builder was Frank Privett and the architect A.E.Cogswell. The only cinema where patrons entered under the screen. An orchestra accompanied silent films. In its last days as a cinema it showed 'Continental' films. It has now been converted into a nightclub in 1981.

30 **Walker, Morley & Co.**, Lead, glass, oil & colour merchants and wholesale ironmongers. Above which were the office for the Portsmouth Times, Hampshire County Times, Isle of Wight Journal and the Newport Times.

26-28 **Borough of Portsmouth Water Company** headquarters. Built in 1883 the architects Rake & Cogswell. The building was renowned for its circular domed stair tower. It closed in 1967 and after brief occupation as a college annexe was demolished in 1970 to make room for the new road, Winston Churchill Avenue.

Here was Hyde Park Road, earlier known as Brunswick Road and now widened and re-aligned as Winston Churchill Avenue.

Pearl Buildings, with copper domes surmounted by cupolas and gabled dormer windows, built in 1899 for the Pearl Assurance Company on the site of Moody's Timber Yard. The architect C.W.Bevis. It was renamed Charter House in 1964. It housed various insurance and legal companies in 88 offices as well as the Washington Hotel (Commercial & Temperance).

Victoria Hotel, listed as a beer retailer in the trade directories from 1865, named the Victoria Arms from 1879 to 1887 and the Victoria Hotel from 1892. It was a Stannard's house. It closed in 1976 and was converted into student accomodation.

Here is St. Pauls Road

The Wiltshire Lamb. One of the early hostelries in the area listed from 1823 in the trade directories. Its address started off as Halfway Houses, then Spring Row, then Landport Road, 12 Commercial Road and finally Hampshire Terrace. There is still a ring for tying up dray horses in the kerb outside. In 1986 it was renamed Drummonds.

Gladstone Buildings. Built in 1885 for the Portsmouth Gladstone Buildings Company by Mr D.W Lewis, the architect was George Rake. The foundation stone was laid by Miss Hilda Baker, daughter of the company chairman Alderman Sir John Baker. The building incorporated the Victoria and Devonshire Halls. The money was provided chiefly by prominent liberals. In the large hall was an organ paid for by subscription in honour of Sir John Baker, leader of Portsmouth Liberal Party for many years. The buildings were demolished in 1961 and replaced by an office block, Mercantile House, now used by the Portsmouth University.

The **Victoria Hall** was designed as a ballroom and was later used as a roller skating rink. The Hall was Portsmouth's first cinema, moving pictures being shown there in 1896. In 1904 Ralph Pringle's North American Film Company were showing films and in 1907 the first talking and singing pictures were

Portsmouth Water Company Offices

shown using Gaumont's singing chrono. The hall became a full time cinema in 1908 with Andrew's Renowned Pictures. From 1920 to 1929 the Cinema Theatre was there, showing in 1925 a De Forest Phonofilm talkie and in 1929 the first full length talkie. Known as the Victoria Hall Cinema from 1930 and after the war until March 1960 as the Victoria Cinema, the last film was 'Expresso Bongo'.

The **Devonshire Hall** had many uses but is best remembered, by the men of the town at least, for a less cheerful use.

"When you joined the army you went there for your medical. You had to go to a different room and a different doctor for different parts of your body. I remember the story about one chap who put Nestles milk in his ear when he went for his medical. He had these runny ears and the doctor couldn't diagnose what was wrong so he got exemption - through Nestles Milk."

"I went down where the old Victoria Hall was and we did a couple of tests. One was to take an ordinary door lock to pieces and putting it back. Everything was over in about an hour, written test and all, for intelligence. We had a medical and we got the 'King's Shilling'. From that moment you were in the army, although we didn't actually join until months later."

"The fruit and vegetable markets have now been tucked tidily away out of sight, the Coliseum, the Hippodrome are gone, the larger part of Commercial Road is pedestrianised and Guildhall Square is deserted after 6 o'clock at night; so what has happened to this once lively and varied street?"

Victoria Hall Cinema, 1910

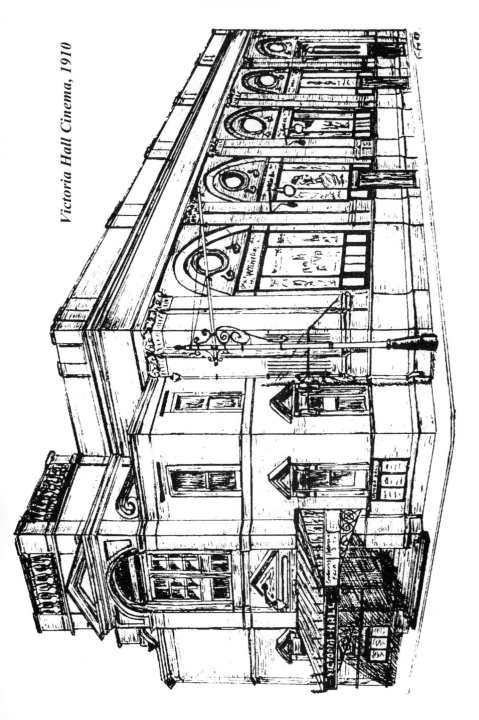

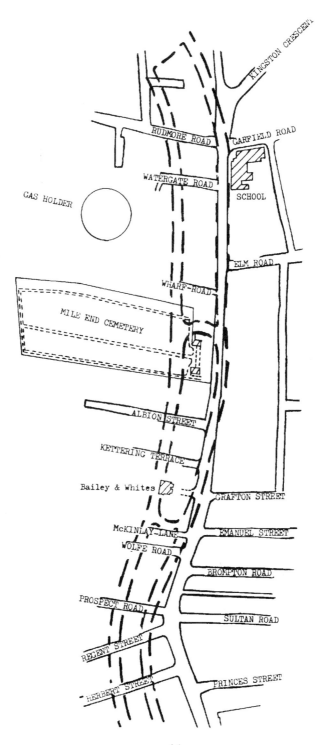

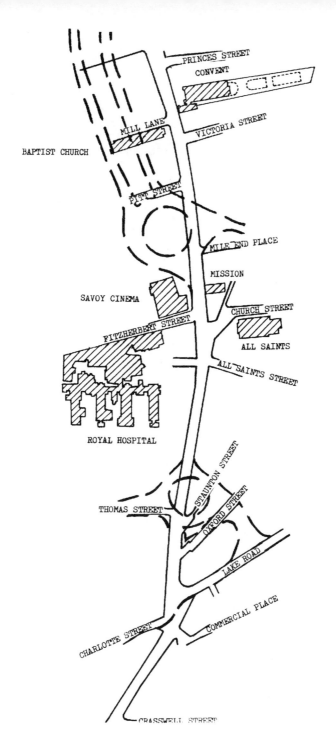

65

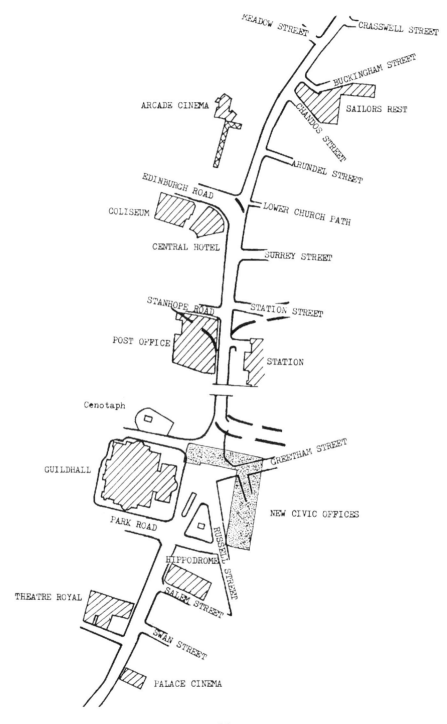

This booklet was compiled by the members of the W.E.A. Local History Group which meets at the North End Adult Learning Centre, Derby Road, North End, Portsmouth. The group is made up of local people who wish to record the history of ordinary peoples' lives and the streets in which they live. The group is very informal and welcomes new members who care to come to Derby Road on a Tuesday evening during term time or write to us.

Class Members at time of original print:
Mr. Albertolli, John Barker, Mr. Bailey, Mrs. Beckett, Leonard Bufton, Celia Clark, Mrs. M. Dalley, Frank Ford, Peter Galvin, Wally Greer, Diane Harris, Bob Haskell, David Jenkins, Stephen Pomeroy, Christine Richards, George Smith and Margaret Webster.

Honorary Members: Don Miles (Typesetting).

Affiliated Members:
Des Beaumont, Morecambe, Lancashire
Vic Burly, Brisbane, Australia
Maggie Munro, Frankstone, Australia

Contributors:
Mr. Cromer, Mr. Gardiner, Mr. Morgan, Mr. Rose, Mrs. Knighton, Mr. Hodge, Mrs. Hansford.

First published in 1985. Revised by Stephen Pomeroy 1994.